101 Essays to Empower You to Live Unstoppable

Frank Agin
Founder & President
AmSpirit Business Connections

ISBN: 978-1-967521-23-4

Published by:
418 Press, A Division of Four Eighteen Enterprises LLC
Post Office Box 30724, Columbus, Ohio 43230-0724

Acknowledgement

In sincere appreciation of Mary Jenkins, founder of Christians Overcoming Cancer (now Cancer Options Collaborative).

Very few people do God's work on Earth, and you are one of them.

I'm blessed to know you.

Table of Contents

Look For These Other Books in This Series

101 Essays to Empower You to Rise & Thrive
101 Essays to Empower You to Up Your Game
101 Essays to Empower You to Build Momentum
101 Essays to Empower You to Limitless Reach
101 Essays to Empower You to Elevate Your Influence
101 Essays to Empower You to Peak Performance
101 Essays to Empower You to The Winning Edge
101 Essays to Empower You to Achieve Greatness
101 Essays to Empower You to Break Barriers

Introduction

This book comes from the insight and creativity of Frank Agin.

Who is Frank? He is the founder and president of AmSpirit Business Connections, an organization that empowers entrepreneurs, sales representatives, and professionals to become successful and gain more referrals through networking.

He is the author of several books, including Foundational *Networking: Building Know, Like and Trust to Create a Lifetime of Extraordinary Success* and *The Three Reasons You Don't Get Referrals*. See all his books and programs at frankagin.com.

Finally, Frank shares information and insights on professional relationships, business networking and best practices for generating referrals on the Networking Rx podcast.

In the summer of 2018, he started planning this short-form podcast. As he mapped out what he wanted to bring to an audience of entrepreneurs, sales representatives, and professionals, he knew he'd have hundreds of programs.

But in addition to all that content, Frank noticed he also had a plethora of other materials—instructive, insightful, and inspirational. All this additional content was worthwhile, but none of it was long enough to create a full episode of Networking Rx.

Not wanting the material to go to waste, Frank developed it into short essays—approximately 150 words each. Then he started to record and share those segments daily under the brand Networking Rx Minutes.

For years, he shared a daily message of empowerment, intuition, and hope. This is a compilation of 100 of those essays. Enjoy.

-1-
Nowhere or Now Here

As motivational speaker, leadership psychologist and author of *The Power of Optimism: Attitude Training for Those Who Want More from Life*, Tim Shurr shares on his podcasts and within his programs, "the difference between the terms 'nowhere' and 'now here' is just adding a space."

Shurr goes on to explain that this is more than just a linguistic sleight of hand, but rather a powerful mindset. You can tell yourself you are nowhere. Or you can tell yourself you are going nowhere. But either will leave you dejected with shoulders slumped and little hope of a brighter tomorrow.

Or you can declare to yourself, "I am now here." In so doing, you get to acknowledge all that you've accomplished. You get to revel in all that you've overcome. You get to take action to improve upon whatever "now here" looks like. And with that you should realize just how special you are.

So, no matter the past, you are now here. Congratulations!

-2-
Like Versus Love

According to Mark Given, author, speaker, and innovator of the trust-based philosophy, "When you're striving to maintain trust, love is critical to achieving superior results. If you like someone, you are glad to see them succeed. But when you love someone you help them succeed. It's really not a lot more complicated than that."

Taking these words to heart, love on the people in your life. For sure, your family and close friends. And, of course, your customers and clients. Ensure that they all enjoy success.

But demonstrating this love does not have to stop there. You can help colleagues succeed, building the business community around you. You can do the same for your vendors, so that they can serve you in a better way. You can even help those you hardly know and serve to make the world a better place.

As Given concludes, "The more you live your life sincerely helping others, the deeper trust grows."

-3-
Stop Chasing Mice

Consider this: A lion is capable of capturing, killing, and eating field mice, as the tiny rodents are everywhere in the world, even on the grassy savannah of Africa. But it turns out that the energy required to do so exceeds the caloric content of the mouse itself. So, a lion that spent its day hunting and eating field mice would slowly starve to death.

A lion cannot live on field mice. A lion needs antelope. Antelope are big animals. While it takes more speed and strength to capture and kill an antelope, once killed, they provide a feast for the lion and her pride.

So, ask yourself this: "Relative to my life and professional pursuits, to what extent am I merely hunting mice?" That is, are you engaged in activities that take more time and energy than the potential positive outcome could ever yield?

If so, stop hunting mice. Rather devote your focus to big-game activities that more fully serve you, as well as others.

-4-
Look for Greatness

Research shows you are more likely to consider yourself successful if you embrace the importance of those around you. This is not an exercise in comparing and contrasting. You know, am I doing better than so-and-so? No. This is a moment of quiet reflection where you acknowledge what others bring to the world.

So, just stop for a moment and think of someone in your life. It doesn't really matter who. Now answer this. What is wonderful about them? Are they funny? Maybe insightful? Driven? Or carefree? What do they bring to life that you admire?

You are, no doubt, some sort of compilation of the people in your life. So, as you consider these notable qualities, ponder just how those things have positively impacted you. Because when you consider the wonderful things about others, you will come to know that that wonder is also in you.

In short, look for the greatness in others and you'll find it in yourself.

-5-

Just Say No

There are only so many days in the week and only so much time in each. You simply cannot do everything. So, you need to make choices. In her book The Intentional Networker, networking and connection expert Patti DeNucci shares her insight on saying NO.

"It can be hard to say no, but to stay true to what's right for you, it's a necessary part of life. There are gracious ways to do it: stand tall, say it like you mean it, keep it short and sweet, and hold fast. No waffling. If you hesitate, you could be persuaded to say yes out of guilt or weakness."

This is the reality: Every decision involves a NO. Think about it. When you say yes to going right, you also say no to going left. So never be afraid of saying no, as you are always saying it already. The key is to step up and say no to the right things to keep you moving forward.

-6-
Multipliers & Dividers

Are you a multiplier or a divider?

A Divider is that person who reluctantly sets a goal, or worse, has a goal imposed on them. Whatever the case, they are resentful of the goal. The Divider adjusts their effort to precisely meet that goal — no more and no less. In their mind the Divider is thinking, "WOW, that deal will get me to quota. Once it closes, I'm going to coast for the rest of the quarter."

A Multiplier, on the other hand, has a whole different approach. They eagerly set goals for themselves and then works tirelessly to achieve them as soon as possible. And when they near the finish line, they drive even harder. The Multiplier says, "WOW! That deal will get me to my goal with a month to spare. I'm going to re-adjust my goal to achieve more."

In a moment of quiet reflection do you tend to behave as a Multiplier or a Divider? Can you guess who achieves more?

-7-
Patience Is Key

In his book *Never Eat Alone*, renowned speaker, author, and marketing consultant Keith Ferrazzi shares:

"The dynamics of building a relationship is necessarily incremental. You can only truly gain someone's trust and commitment little by little over time. In this fast-paced, instant-gratification, gottta-have-it-now world patience is a challenge. Especially, when there are quotas to meet and bills to pay. The outside demands of a professional life do not and cannot alter the inside realities of building relationships."

Ferrazzi's point is an important one. As much as you want people to come to know, like and trust you on your terms, you simply cannot control that timeline. Yes, you can do things to help the process, but the process works on its own pace.

Moreover, that pace varies from person to person and circumstance to circumstance. Therefore, in the end, the most important element of building relationships is time. And for that reason, patience is key.

-8-
Three Underlying Premises

In her book, *Cultivate: The Power of Winning Relationships*, sought-after leadership and executive development expert Morag Barrett shares three underlying premises to cultivating winning relationships.

Premise 1: The world of work is a team sport. Barrett calls professional work the toughest team sport of all. And yet, she acknowledges that often there is more infighting than teamwork. Commit to being a team player no matter your role or the size of your team.

Premise 2: You are dependent upon others for your success. Barrett shares that a solo mindset can be the hero in the short term, but not over the long haul. Any worthwhile professional life is a challenge, and you need the people around you to help.

Premise 3: Relationships matter. Barrett implies that you need to be intentional about cultivating and developing relationships and this needs to be a priority. In short, you need to make time for it and endeavor to do it well.

-9-
Networking Smarter

Consider this: There are only 24 hours in a day. At least half of these we devote to personal time – family, sleeping or other matters. A large chuck of the balance is devoted to actually being productive – so-called "working for a living." The remainder – which is only a few hours – is yours to be networking.

Becoming better networked is not a matter of finding more time to interact with others. There is only so much time in the day. Rather, to become better networked you need to be more efficient with your precious networking time.

For this reason, you're best to find opportunities to add value, rather than just being a face in the crowd. And you should always be open to finding ways to build relationships with others, no matter what your relationship is now.

The point is, to become better networked, you need to network smarter in the moment rather than trying to find more moments to network.

-10-
The Most Valuable, Least Expensive

Building relationships is the most valuable activity you can undertake. Like it or not, your status in life, as well as all that you aspire to achieve, is pinned to other people in your life.

It's what they do that ultimately makes a difference – their introductions, the opportunities they provide, the information they share, as well as the encouragement and support they give. Yes, building relationships is the most valuable activity you can undertake.

And while it's the most valuable activity, it's also one of – if not the - least expensive. For example, offering compliments to others is a marvelous way to improve someone's self-esteem and bring them closer to you. And it literally costs you nothing to do it.

The same goes for introducing someone you know to key contacts for them. Or sharing information. Or alerting them to opportunities. Or cheering them on when they need it. Or just lending them a sympathetic ear. All of this serves to build valuable relationships and yet costs nothing.

-11-
It's Not About the Result

In the book *Becoming Competition Proof: Stand Out and Overcome Competition Through Generosity, Service and Added Value*, adventure coach Berta Medina-Garcia encourages you to make mutually beneficial introductions. She indicates that this is an effective means of staying top of mind, adding value to your network and amplifying others.

She goes on to offer this caution when making these connections: "Don't be tied to the result."

In other words, it's your responsibility to empower two strangers to become associated, but nothing more. Garcia goes on to explain that "All of my introduction e-mails end with 'I will let you take it from here.' This means the ball is in their court and it's up to them to determine what they are going to do with it."

In short, you have permission to not be concerned with what will come from a connection. In fact, you don't need to ensure that they connect at all. Your job is merely to make the introduction.

-12-
Relationships As Chess

On the *Networking Rx* podcast, Kwame Christian, negotiation expert and author of the book *Finding Confidence In Conflict*, shared that "All relationships are a never-ending game of chess."

He went on to indicate that like chess, relationships have certain rules. There are acceptable ways to engage with others. You can only control 50% of the activity. And there are topics that are off limits.

Likewise, both involve strategy. Sometimes you're more aggressive in your approach, creating reactions by your moves. Other times you're more passive, allowing things to come to you.

And finally, relationships require give and take. Just as you sometimes need to sacrifice a particular chess piece to enhance your position, in relationships not everything is going to go your way. Sometimes you have to purposefully concede on something, even though you'd rather not.

Christian creates a compelling analogy, whether you fully understand the board game or not. Relationships are like chess. They both require discipline of thought and intentionality of action.

-13-
Out Fly the Crows

The only bird that will peck at an eagle is the crow. These cackling black birds will sit on the back of the eagle and bite at the neck of these majestic birds. The eagle doesn't respond to the crow. And it doesn't retaliate. It neither wastes the time nor the energy.

Rather, the beautiful and powerful eagle simply opens its wings and begins to rise higher and higher in the sky, taking the crow for a ride. The higher the flight, however, the harder it is for the crow to breathe. Eventually the crow falls due to lack of oxygen.

Like the eagle, you have crows in your life, too. Naysayers. And time wasters. Undisciplined souls. And individuals who seem to wonder aimlessly. Don't waste your time with these crows.

Rather aspire to great heights. And work tirelessly to get there. The crows in your world won't be able to keep pace and will slowly fall away. And you will achieve a beautiful and majestic existence.

-14-
Improving Mutual Understanding

In her book *Rainmaker Roadmap: A Step-by-Step Guide to Building a Prosperous Business,* marketing consultant Kimberly Rice helps her readers become better conversationalists by breaking down four active listening tactics.

First, clarifying. This involves asking a communication partner to elaborate upon something they've said by offering more information.

Second, paraphrasing. Rice indicates this is the practice of repeating your communication partner's message in your own words to ensure that you're on the same page.

Third, reflecting. She explains that this is more than just clarifying, but also conveying the underlying feelings to the message.

And, finally, summarizing. This is the act of reviewing and re-capping major points from the conversation.

Listening is the most important part of conversation. Taking deliberate steps to incorporate these active listening tactics into your conversations will ensure that you improve the mutual understanding, as well as helping to create and cultivate productive relationships.

-15-
The Seeds of Altruism

In his book, *Winning Without Intimidation*, Bob Burg discusses the fine act of thoughtfulness, which is the foundation of generosity. Burg indicates that although this does not necessarily come naturally, being thoughtful is a simple idea that requires no incredible skills.

He goes on to share that thoughtfulness can be as simple as holding a door open for someone, paying a well-deserved compliment, or leaving those prime parking spaces for someone else.

Burg tells us that these acts of thoughtfulness may or may not be noticed but that doesn't really matter. What does matter is that you continue to be thoughtful. If nothing else, this will warm your soul with good feelings. Moreover, these acts are the seeds of altruism. That is, from these simple gestures more meaningful acts of kindness sprout. And as they do, you grow in stature, in time becoming forever branded as a person of generosity. And this is all just an extension of your thoughtfulness.

-16-
The Asking Warm & Fuzzy Feeling

No doubt, you are an accomplished human being. You have valuable experiences, knowledge, and insight that you've accumulated over the years. Be generous with it. Right now, someone is aspiring to your place in life. And your advice or mentorship could really help.

Now answer this: How do you feel when someone asks you for this sort of support or assistance? Is it fair to say you feel flattered, acknowledged, and honored? Very likely! It's a warm and fuzzy feeling, right? After all, they've thought enough of you to believe that you could be of assistance. And they've acknowledged that you've achieved a degree of success.

Now, use this information to your advantage. How? Simple. Ask someone you aspire to for advice or assistance. In so doing, you'll acknowledge their greatness, flatter them and make them feel great. By asking, you'll get some help, and they'll get a warm and fuzzy feeling. And so, in the end, you both win.

-17-
Rise Like a Champion

Professional tennis player Serena Williams, winner of 23 Grand Slam singles titles, is credited with saying: "I really think a champion is defined not by their wins, but by how they can recover when they fall."

Everyone falls down. Everyone. Not everyone recovers the same, however. Some stay down, not willing to tumble again. Some get back up, but then devote time and energy to making excuses or blaming others. And still others become jaded by the experience, carrying on as if the world has conspired against them.

But the true champions that Williams alludes to are those who don't just get up. When they get up, they stand tall … throw their shoulders back … and raise their chin high. No, they don't like to fall, but they accept it as a part of process.

Whoever you are, accept that you're going to fall. Some falls will be big and others small. Whatever the case, when you do fall, rise like a champion.

-18-
The True Spirit of Networking

Networking gets a bad rap. Certainly, there are those who deploy abusive tactics in the name of it. But networking has nothing to do with poor salesmanship. In fact, it is the opposite.

The true spirit of networking is about giving of your resources, time, and talent. It is about helping and not looking back with wonder or expectation of "What's in it for me?"

The true spirit of networking is about helping simply because it is the right thing to do. Certainly, you want to believe that the goodness you have heaped onto the world will make it back to you somehow. That's fine.

But the true spirit of networking is about helping others wherever you can, whenever you can, and never worrying about what it means for you. After all, in the true spirit of networking you need to remember that it is not how you help others that matters. What matters is the spirit that moves you.

-19-
Share Your Smile

Smile. You see, when you smile, powerful psychological forces kick into gear. In fact, science shows that when you grin you tend to have an enhanced mood.

But science also show that when you smile people cannot help but smile back. And by getting them to smile you've empowered them to feel better. And because you've boosted their mood, they tend to carry on that grin long after you're gone.

And so, with that smile, when they encounter others your smile is subconsciously passed on – along with all the goodness that goes with it. And thus, they continue to smile, spreading your silly little smirk from one person to the next and the next.

If you think about it, it's entirely possible that your smile could make its way all around the world and back. So, tomorrow when you're not quite feeling it and someone smiles at you, that smile might really be yours from yesterday. So, smile.

-20-
Slow and Steady Wins

Author, speaker, and personal development influencer Lewis Howes remarked in his book *The School of Greatness*:

"If there is one thing you should take from this book about pursuing your vision and achieving your dreams, it should be this: You can go as slow as you need to go, but you cannot stop. You can never give up or drop out of giving your best in your life."

Howes goes on to indicate that success is not easy. No one said it would be. Nor should it be. And no one said it would be achieved overnight. But the reality is that you never actually fail unless you simply stop doing something. Anything.

Yes, life is full of setbacks. And yes, some days will be better than others. But, today, if you're willing to take just one little step towards your goals – and then another tomorrow and then another the day after and so on – then you absolutely will not fail. Slow and steady wins.

-21-
Beyond Initial Contact

At networking events, take the initiative to connect with others. You know, make eye contact, smile, and say hello. Sure, sometimes this will lead to nothing. So what? Don't take it personally. Often enough, however, people stop and indicate that they are interested in expanding the initial contact into a more meaningful connection.

When this happens, ensure to do these three things: One, offer your hand in anticipation of a handshake. And be sure to make it a solid one. Not a bone crusher or a limb fish either. Keep in mind that this is your true first impression.

Two, as you shake hands, offer your name and be sure to enunciate your first name clearly. This helps them know you, as well as cueing them to offer their name in return.

And three, when they offer their name clarify it aloud. "It's great to meet you. Susan, right?" This will help you remember their name as well as subtly imply that their name is important to you.

-22-
Practice the Connection

Andrew Chiodo, in his book *The Fine Art of Networking*, states: "If you were to talk to 100 'great networkers,' you might have a terrific shock when fifty of them say 'I had and still have a fear of talking to strangers, so I do a lot of practicing.'"

Thousands upon thousands of years ago, humans lived in clans or tribes of 150 or so. And throughout their lives, they never saw another human outside of their group. If they did, it generally wasn't a good thing, as it was likely a precursor to an invasion or raid. So, humans learned to associate strangers with bad things.

Fast forward to the 21st century and much of that ancient hardwiring is still intact. So, everyone has a subconscious fear of strangers.

You can, however, be more comfortable connecting with new people through repetition. Like anything, practice connecting will quell your natural apprehension. And this is the first step to turning previous strangers into future great friends.

-23-
Cycle of Healing

In her book, The Light in 9/11: Shocked by Kindness, Healed By Love author Lisa Luckett shares:

"From my 9/11 experience I've identified a cycle of giving and receiving. The logic to gracefully let others help you in order to help themselves is very clear to me now. If we keep others from helping in our time of pain or crisis, we are blocking them from receiving the soul food they, too, desperately need. Human beings need to help each other. It is hardwired in our DNA.

In our chaotic and unstable world – from an angry Mother Nature to devastating national and world events – it is likely that one day each of us will need help. When that happens, I encourage you to embrace the notion that not only is it good to give but it is also good to receive. This exchange is a healthy and necessary cycle of healing."

-24-
The Formula

Establishing a productive network is something that is entirely formula driven, like mixing a drink. That is, if you do certain things, a productive network will follow.

Given that, the prescribed formula for creating a productive network dictate that you take responsibility to do the following:

Create a series of basic relationships with people you can know, like and trust.

Nurture those relationships with genuine care and concern.

Make a sincere attempt to help those around you.

Educate those relationships with how they can help you become more successful.

And demonstrate patience, knowing that eventually good things will result.

Certainly, this formula is not as simple as mixing a whiskey sour or making a screwdriver. Sometimes you need to do more educating than nurturing and sometimes patience is the main ingredient. Despite these potential complexities, it is, nonetheless, a formula.

In summary, if you want a productive network, you simply need to devote your energies to working the formula.

-25-
Out of the Comfort Zone

At the front of the novel *Out of The Comfort Zone*, there is a poem that reads:

"We live in a zone of comfort -- situations that threaten us, we tend to avoid.

"When we're hurting, we seek consolation; when we're tired, we rest; and when we're outmatched, we concede.

"But still somewhere within us, we have the concentration to ignore the deepest pain; the strength to endure the most exhausting fatigue; and the means to conquer even the impossible challenge.

"In essence, through courage, hard work and discipline, we have the ability to leave this zone of comfort.

"Only here can we discover our true potential.

"Although testing the limits of our potential doesn't guarantee fame, fortune or championship status, it's Out of the Comfort Zone where winning begins."

This piece makes you ponder, doesn't it? Where are you pushing yourself? And where might you be playing it safe? Step outside your comfort zone today. It's the only way you can win at whatever you do.

-26-
The Comeback Set-Up

Tim Shurr, motivational speaker, leadership psychologist and author of *The Power of Optimism: Attitude Training for Those Who Want More from Life*, shares on his podcasts and within his programs, "A setback is just a set-up for a comeback."

Shurr's mantra is insightful and there is evidence of it all around. Companies have great years following one or two where they've stumbled. Sports teams tend to have their best performances following a loss. And history is filled with figures who's most shining moments were preceded by a tumultuous time.

Why is this the case? For one, setbacks provide a great opportunity to reflect upon prior performances and find ways to improve. People simply don't learn as much from successes. Additionally, life's stumbling blocks serve as inspiration to double down on effort and persistence, whereas success can lead to complacency.

So, if you're experiencing a rough patch, take note. Life may just be setting you up for a great comeback.

-27-
The Strength of the Network

In his book *The Jungle Book*, English journalist, short-story writer, poet, and novelist Rudyard Kipling shared the line: "The strength of the pack is the wolf, and the strength of the wolf is the pack." Certainly, this relates to a group of wolves in nineteenth century India who took in and raised a young boy, but the line also has application to you.

The strength of your network is you. After all, you bring to it your experiences, a wealth of information, as well as connections to a variety of opportunities and countless additional contacts. Without you, your network is weaker and nowhere near what it is.

At the same time, your strength comes from your network. You rely on it for a wealth of information. Likewise, your stature in life is a result of contacts and opportunities from your network. Without your network, you would not be the person you are, nor the person you could be.

-28-
Playing The "IF"

Do you know what all successful people have in common? They all play the "IF."

What is the "IF"? Well, it might be easier to describe what it's not. Too often corporate America, public service sectors, and most every career operates like this: "I'm coming to work, and you'll need to pay me X." This is "Playing the Promise."

Successful people don't work that way. Rather, they operate more like this: "If I can find reasonably suitable people to contact ... and if I can get them to listen ... and if they like what I have to offer ... and if I'm able to package it all more attractively than my competition ... well, then, I just might be able to get X."

While there are no guarantees, playing the "IF" is extremely fulfilling in lots of ways. Mainly, when you play the "IF," the rewards you get are more closely aligned with the work you expend.

-29-
"Once I" Syndrome

On the Networking Rx podcast, Renée Piane, an award-winning international relationship reinvention expert, inspirational speaker, and author of the books "*Love Mechanics*" and "*Get Real About Love*," shared about what she refers to as the "once I" syndrome.

She explained that far too often she watches as people put off trying to find that special relationship in their lives, saying, "I'll focus on my love life once I ..." You can complete that sentence with any number of excuses.

Unfortunately, the "once I" syndrome is not limited to those putting off finding romance. It also impacts those looking for less-intimate relationships. You might hear: "I'll connect with others once my business is more established ... once I get my website done ... once I have a clear vision for myself." And this list can go on and on.

This is the reality: All the things you need in life come from your network. Given that, ditch the "once I" mantra and start allowing others into your life.

-30-
You Can't Tickle Yourself

Scientists have shown that people can't tickle themselves. It's true. A scientific fact, if you will. The human brain distinguishes between "expected" and "unexpected" sensations. Thus, when individuals attempt to tickle themselves, the brain will not allow the tickling sensation to occur from this expected touch.

Just as individuals cannot tickle themselves, a person cannot experience true joy when they know that a gift is coming. Your generosity is most effective when you sneak up on someone to present it.

Your spouse or significant other is romantically moved when you give them a card and gift when they least expect it. Your compliments have a special meaning when you give them without any sort of forewarning. Likewise, the referrals you give, and the business contacts you create for others become extraordinary acts of giving when you do them without any sort of notice.

Therefore, to truly build relationships, on occasion you need to get out there and tickle someone – metaphorically speaking, of course.

-31-
The Fog of War

Long before he was President, Dwight D. Eisenhower was a general in the army and is credited with saying this: "In preparing for battle I have always found that plans are useless, but planning is indispensable."

Eisenhower was referring to something military strategists call "the fog of war." Once a battle begins, information that is tactically relevant can become confusing and even distorted. Because of the difficulty of seeing patterns in the midst of this fog, tactical leaders are taught to act independently of operational plans.

No, life shouldn't be violent, but it is often characterized as war. Others out there want what you already have. If you want to keep what you've got – clients, a job, or a place in the community – you need to have a plan to keep it.

But in executing on your plan, know that at times things can seem complicated and you'll feel like you're in a fog. In these moments, there is no shame in improvising.

-32-
Invisible But Invaluable

In one of his weekly newsletters, Mark Given, author, speaker, and innovator of the trust-based philosophy, related his thoughts as he drove to visit the graves of his close family members. He shared:

"They had been on my mind, and as I stood there and looked at their stones, I reflected on how valuable they had been to me while they were alive ... and even today.

"Each of them may be invisible now, but they still continue to be invaluable.

They have made my life better and easier because of the things they taught me.

They represented goodness and honesty and trust. Each of them was a wonderful example of what I want to become."

Given goes on to remind that you, too, will be invisible someday. He then encourages you to ponder the value you bring to the world. In short, what are you doing today to help assure that you are invaluable once you are no longer here.

-33-
Special People

Much of the world never puts themselves out there. They play it safe. They live in their comfort zone. They don't try new things. They only embark on things they know. That's much of the world. And it only aspires to mediocrity.

However, that's not everyone. There is another a thin margin of people. They are the brave. They take chances. They accept being in uncomfortable situations. They'll venture into something different for the challenge. They venture into something different because others need them to. These are special people.

Unfortunately, from time to time these special people meet with failures, disappointments, and setbacks. It's just a reality of living life outside the comfort zone.

These moments of heartache don't make these people less special. No. It is these exact moments that serve to make these people extraordinary. Because these are the people who will move forward despite the set-back – standing tall, shoulders back and chin held high – ready to take on the next challenge.

-34-
Nickels & Dimes

Networking is not about making big, calculated moves on special occasions. Rather, networking is about doing ordinary thing. Doing ordinary things, reasonably well, consistently, time after time.

In practical terms, it's about connecting with strangers and, in time, making them friends. And it's about cultivating relationships with friends and keeping them on your radar. It's about making small talk around seemingly nothing, yet having the conversation seems to mean everything. It's about adding value whenever you can, but never expecting value in return.

It's about a lot of little things but nothing spectacular or special. Rather, it's about the simple things – consistent simple things day after day, week after week and month after month.

It's not akin to garnering a handful of hundred- or thousand-dollar bills in those unique moments when all the stars align. Rather, networking is like simply earning nickels and dimes, over and over, no matter the circumstances.

-35-
Pro Bono Publicist

In his book *Business Beyond Business: How to Gain Magnetic Influence, Meaningful Connection and Profitable Publicity by Becoming a Radically Generous Entrepreneur*, consultant and author Paul Edwards advocates becoming a pro bono publicist.

Edwards essentially shares that a great way to add value to others is to go out of your way to promote them. For starters, you can make an effort on social media to like, comment and share posts made by others. Moreover, you can highlight those same people in the things you post. And you can make recommendations on LinkedIn, Google, and other platforms.

Outside of social media, when meeting with one person, look for opportunities to share about and promote others, highlighting their work and how it served you well.

In reality, becoming a pro bono publicist costs you absolutely nothing. And all it requires is a little forethought and a willingness to do something for someone else. The lasting goodwill it creates, however, is monumental.

-36-
Stretch Like a Balloon

Balloons are great. Blow air into one. It'll take some effort, but the balloon expands and grows. Ppuusshh air into it again and it'll grow more. And more. And more. Then when you let it go, the air comes rushing out as the balloon whips around the room.

When you catch up to it, the balloon appears to have reverted to its original form. But when you blow air into it again, you'll find it doesn't take nearly the same effort to get it to expand and grow. It's the same balloon, you've just loosened its elasticity.

This is like committing to personal and professional development. Getting started takes effort. Deciding which direction to go is not easy. Knowing who has worthwhile material takes some exploration. And getting through the initial foundation material can be tiresome.

But once done, you've loosened the elasticity of learning. The effort becomes easier, and the results seem more worthwhile, as your mind and abilities expand and grow.

-37-
Beyond Know, Like & Trust

The foundation of any network is getting others to know, like and trust you. But this is only the foundation. If you want your network to move beyond this into the realm of really being productive, you must do more.

Remember, when people come to know, like and trust you they're only at a point where they have a desire to help you achieve and succeed. It doesn't mean that they know how.

So, the next step beyond this foundation is one of education. You must teach and inform your network on how to recognize things that could benefit you. They need to know what opportunities you seek. What information you need to advance your mission. And who the people are you'd like to meet.

In short, to be successful via networking, you need to move beyond know, like and trust.

-38-
Four Great Attitude Strategies

There is little question that any reasonable person would prefer to associate with someone with a positive, forward-focused attitude than with someone who is continually glum and downtrodden.

That's a no brainer. What's not, however, is getting your mindset appropriately established and keeping it there. Gary Wilbers, author of *Cultivate Positive Culture: 10 Actions To Faithful Living*, offers four strategies to help ensure you consistently have a great attitude.

One, show gratitude daily. Afterall, being thankful attracts good things to you.

Two, expose yourself to motivational material. It's those positive notions that will play like a soundtrack in your mind.

Three, journal your thoughts. This creates an awareness to moments when your mindset might be slipping.

And four, exercise. A moderate daily regimen will lift your spirits.

Remember your attitude works within a range and you control where the meter points. Thus, do what you can to keep the meter pointing high.

-39-
Small Talk Is BIG

Never underestimate the power of small talk. Every good connection started with it, as this seemingly mundane chitchat bridged the divide between stranger and friend. And every relationship relies on it extensively to serve as an ongoing reminder as to why people associate with one another.

Sure, at some point you need to generate referrals and close business, because a charming smile doesn't pay the rent. But like anything worthwhile in life, things need to proceed in their proper order. And they can only move at a certain pace.

It's the role of small talk to get things started, as everything has a beginning. And small talk is the gravity that holds relationships together as they ebb and flow.

So, while a witty introduction or some profound insight is nice, there is nothing shameful about a mundane comment to break the ice. Something as simple as, "This is great coffee!" or, "Did you see the game last night?" The point is, small talk is big.

-40-
Hanging On By A Finger

Life is not easy. Life is not fair. And life is not simple. One day, you might have a clear sense as to how it could unfold. And then despite all your planning and hard work, fate has other plans for you.

Consider the case of Trevor Wikre. As a senior football player at Mesa State University, he had high hopes of seeing through his final year of collegiate football, graduating, and then moving on with life.

Unfortunately, he was hit with a terrible dilemma. You see, in an early season practice he suffered a horrific injury to his pinky finger. The injury was so severe that he had a choice: Not play football or risk losing his injured finger. He opted for football, having the finger surgically amputated.

While you might not have made the same choice, know this: Life will throw difficult choices at you. Get used to it. And be ready to step up and decide what's best for you.

-41-
Second Wind

On his blog, sports psychologist Dr. Rob Bell shares about second winds – that period of revitalization in athletics where you move past the initial sluggish movement and labored breathing.

Bell reminds us that we have second winds in life, too. This is when you finally hit your stride professionally. Renewed confidence. And achieving results, where there was frustration before.

As Bell shares, the key (in both athletics and professional life) is to survive long enough through the period of anxiety and discomfort that you can enjoy the flow of the second wind. He offers four insights for getting to this point.

One, know your why. With that, you can come up with the appropriate how.

Two, don't stop. He reminds, "even slow walkers arrive," so just don't quit.

Three, find your rhythm. Everything has a tempo. Find yours. Not someone else's. Yours.

And four, patience. Your second wind in life is coming. Believe it and commit to hanging on long enough to enjoy it.

-42-
Building a Wonderful Habit

Everyone knows that "thank you", "thanks", or similar words are common expressions of gratitude. And most understand their usefulness in expressing sincere appreciation for a job well done, kind words spoken, or some magnanimous deed.

And yet, as straightforward as those notions are, words of thanks tend to be shared far too infrequently.

Perhaps people are busy. Perhaps they simply forget. Perhaps they aren't quite clued into the importance of appreciation. Whatever the case, do not be that person.

The reality is that everything is worthy of thanks. Every word. Every gesture. Everything. Even encounters that might not seem so pleasant are worthy of appreciation. You simply need to take the time and have the grace to look for the value you can derive.

So, you can and should thank people for any and everything. Moreover, if you go out of your way to say thanks, it will become a wonderful habit and you'll never overlook doing it.

-43-
You Are the Expert

Everyone has competition. Including you. That's just a fact of professional life. But another reality is this: Most people don't do what you do.

Think about it. While it might seem like lots of people are operating in your space, it's really only a small sliver of the entire population. As such, the vast majority of people don't compete with you. Moreover, few people really know as much about your business, industry, or profession as you do. Very, very few!

So, as you conduct yourself within your community (however you define it), you should feel emboldened to carry yourself with a certain swagger. One that serves to say, "I am the expert." Speak with authority. Know that you add value to the world, no matter what business you're in.

Remember, this is not some false bravado. Few people know your world like you do. So, stand tall and be assured of your place. That confidence, in the end, will result in a bigger following for you.

-44-
Splashing With Personalized Gifts

A staple of building relationships is staying top of mind with those you know. Certainly, you can do that with periodic interactions. But you can also achieve this by splashing those you care about with an occasional gift. What might these gifts be?

Referral coach Matt Ward discussed this topic in his book, *MORE: Word of Mouth Referrals, Lifelong Customers & Raving Fans*. He said:

"If you think about the most meaningful gifts you have received, it's likely the ones that took into account your personality, passions, and interests – that were customized to you. When you consider giving a gift to a contact, use your heart and mind to think of something that will be meaningful to them. Be intentional with your gift."

To find what's meaningful, Ward suggests that you pay attention to your contact through conversations in-person or via e-mail. He also recommends that you examine their social media and other online content for clues.

As a little tip: Matt Ward love bacon!

-45-
See Through Their Perspective

The most important part of communication is not what you have to say. And it's not necessarily just about getting the other person talking. Rather, what matters most is the effort you put into understanding what the other person has to say.

According to Dr. David Niven's book, *The 100 Simple Secrets of Successful People*, research has shown that good listeners are more likely to attempt to see things through the perspective of the other person.

Use this research to your advantage. Afterall, making eye contact and politely listening, is nice. But it's not enough. You need to invest yourself in what others are saying. You need to take an active role in listening and truly understand. This requires not just understanding the words but developing an awareness as to the passion with which they are spoken.

Furthermore, this involves recognizing how their message fits into the bigger picture of their world. It's this seeing through their perspective that draws them closer to you and builds the relationship.

-46-
Choose Your Own Path

You're surrounded by well-meaning people who offer up advise and suggestions. And, no doubt, they do it with the best of intentions. Listen to it. Take it in. Compare ideas. Weight your options carefully.

But in the end, trust your intuition. And don't put too much emphasis on what others might advise, as compared to your own sense. The fact is that no matter how well-meaning they might be, they don't know your situation like you do. And you could never explain the passion that's in your heart. So, no one knows better than yourself what's right for you.

Wherever you ultimately land in life, you will be judged on your own merits. Whatever you achieve will be largely a result of your own actions. And whenever something doesn't work out, you'll be given little consolation for the advice or suggestions you did or didn't take along the way. In the end, it's up to you, so choose your own path.

-47-
The Q v. Q Debate

In his book, *Be Connected: Strategies To Attract The Right Opportunities, Connections And Clients Through Effective Networking*, social architect Terry Bean discusses the debate between the quantity and quality strategies to building a network.

In one corner there is quantity: The tactic where you willingly connect with anyone and everyone - being ever ready to add another to your network. In the other corner there is quality: The policy where you only build your network with those with whom you've developed a minimum level of mutual trust.

Which is the better approach? According to Bean, both. He shares that you shouldn't choose between one or the other to be your all-in, one-and-only approach. After all, building a social media following is entirely different than creating a stable of trusted vendors, valuable clients, and resourceful colleagues.

Rather he encourages that you rely on each strategy, depending upon what you're trying to achieve. That wins the Q v. Q debate every time.

-48-
The Golden Opportunity

What is a Golden Opportunity? It is that break that has a life-altering impact on your business, career, or personal life.

Consider Harrison Ford – discovered by George Lucas as he labored as a carpenter in the movie industry. Have you ever wondered where Ford would be today if he had not been pounding nails on the set when Lucas happened through? Or better still, have you ever wondered who would have gotten the part of Han Solo in the original *Star Wars* trilogy?

Out there – somewhere – for you, is someone that possesses a Golden Opportunity. Again, it's that chance meeting or conversation that will result in a break that will wonderfully impact your entire world. Who holds this for you? Or where do you find it?

Well, you just never know. Which means that you need to treat everyone you know and everyone you meet as if they are the person who can provide your Golden Opportunity.

.

-49-
Perfectly Imperfect

You are not perfect. No one is. But before you go changing, consider this.

Barbara Streisand is one of the most acclaimed singers and actors of all time. And she did it despite having a nose that many considered unappealing. Sure, with her fame and wealth she could have had it fixed. But why? Perhaps she could have achieved more if cosmetic surgery inched her towards perfection.

But by not doing so, her appearance served as a rebellious stance against the demands of show business. It branded her as a free spirit. And that is part of what makes Streisand iconic.

Sure, you should look to improve. Become more appreciative of others. Set loftier goals. And maybe go easier on junk food. But like Streisand, some aspects of your imperfections are just you. And to change them, might change the very essence of who you are.

In short, simply accept certain aspects of yourself, as they serve to make you perfectly imperfect.

-50-
Horizon of Achievement

Dr. Adam Grant, Wharton School of Business psychology professor and best-selling author, shared on Twitter:

"One reason why so many high achievers are unhappy: their expectations rise faster than their accomplishments. Success is most satisfying when you have high aspirations but modest expectations. You can set ambitious goals without taking it for granted that you'll attain them."

In one simple tweet, Grant encourages you to dream big. And act big. But at the same time feel no shame if things don't work out exactly as you'd planned.

Yes, have ambitious goals. But remember that while much of achieving them is in your control, a percentage is not. Achievements, to a degree, hinges on situations and circumstances that just might stymie the end result you'd hoped for.

The most successful and most fulfilled are those who are satisfied with what they achieve. And they realize that what they really want is somewhere on a horizon that they may never quite reach.

-51-
Business Card Foreplay

Building a relationship from that first initial contact can seem like a precarious moment. After all, if it's at a networking event or business afterhours, you might only have 15-20 minutes to get a toehold into their life. You know, the beginning senses of mutual know, like, and trust.

One aspect of this is getting their business card, so you're empowered with their information to follow up. And at the same time, you want to ensure they have yours. Certainly, once you offer yours, they will likely reciprocate. But you can't do this right out of the gate.

So as not to be perceived as too pushy, before you hand out your business cards you should establish a conversation with the prospect first. Get the conversation started with innocent, but important small talk and then naturally migrate to more professional conversation. Once engaged in this portion of the conversation, the situation will be more comfortable for you to offer your business card.

-52-
One Step Closer

You want to get better networked. So, you contemplate the dozens of people in your network. Who would be the best person to reach out to? You walk into an event and there is a sea of one-hundred or more new faces. Who do you attempt to get acquainted with? You log onto LinkedIn and come up with thousands upon thousands of potential new contacts with whom to network. Where do you even start?

No question, trying to determine who you should focus on can feel daunting. Remember, however, there are seven billion people on the planet. And somehow you are connected to every one of them.

So, who do you connect with? The reality is that it really doesn't matter. No contact is truly a bad one. In fact, every connection gets you one step closer to the contacts you need or the opportunities you hope for. Given that, don't be concerned with where you begin. Rather, simply commit to getting started on the networking process.

-53-
The Long-Term Sacrifice

Retired U.S. Marine Corps Lieutenant General George J. Flynn shared in the foreword of Simon Sinek's book *Leaders Eat Last: Why Some Teams Pull Together and Other's Don't*: "Great leaders truly care about those they are privileged to lead and understand that the true cost of leadership privilege comes at the expense of self-interest."

To elaborate on Flynn's words, the human mind can only work on one thought at a time. So, you're either focused on advancing yourself or focused on advancing others. You can't concentrate on both.

Sure, centering on yourself will bring short-term success. But going that route, no one will consider you a leader. To be a leader, you need to become selfless. You need to sacrifice focusing on yourself and devote time and attention to those you serve.

While this might seem shortsighted, it's not. Because as a leader, when you focus on others, they will focus on you in return. And that's where the sacrifice yields a long-term pay off.

-54-
All Or None

Jim Clear, bestselling author of the book *Atomic Habits*, shared a story in the articles section of his website that is paraphrased like this:

An anthropologist, studying the culture of an African tribe, proposed a game to the boys and girls. He put a basket of fruit near a tree. Then he gathered the children some distance away. Attempting to tap into their competitive nature, the anthropologist told them that the first one to get to the fruits would get them all.

When he turned them loose, something interesting happened: The boys and girls all took each other's hands and ran together. This would ensure that no one would win and that they would all enjoy the fruit together.

As they did, the befuddled anthropologist asked them why they ran like. Why didn't anyone of them try to claim the fruit for themselves? One girl spoke for the group, stating, "How can one of us be happy if all the other ones are sad?"

-55-
Moving On Gracefully

As wonderful as chatting with a great new contact at a networking event is, be sure to reserve time to get acquainted with others. Talk with them for 15-20 minutes, get their contact information and pledge to get back to them.

This will allow you the opportunity to meet and connect with other people. To this end, when you find a lull in the conversation, simply suggest to your great new contact:

"I would love to keep talking, but ...

"I don't want to occupy your whole time;" Or,

"There are a couple of other people I need to connect with before the event is over;" Or,

"I promised myself that I would meet three great new contacts today ... you make one and now I need to find the other two." Or,

"If you don't mind, however, I want to reconnect later to find a time to continue this conversation."

This strategy will allow you the opportunity to meet and connect with other people.

-56-
Play Ball

In his book *Small Ball, Big Results*, Kansas City Royals broadcaster Joel Goldberg shares an early lesson he received from another broadcaster. This veteran to the industry chided: "Win or lose, you have a role to play and a job to do."

Goldberg shared that he has relied on that message to drive him to success as part of the Kansas City Royals' broadcast team for over a decade. But it's a great message for you too.

You have great days. Days that are the equivalent of a championship win in baseball. Congratulations! You must quickly refocus, however. Your life doesn't end there. The competition to succeed continues. And if you're not careful you will lose what you've gained.

Likewise, you also have setbacks of various kinds. Whatever they are and no matter how they impact you, you need to soldier on. No one is going to stop life to feel sorry for you. In baseball terms: Get back up. Dust yourself off. And play ball!

-57-
Today's Plan

In the book The Little BIG Things: 163 Ways to Pursue Excellence, author Tom Peters shares a story about a man approaching JP Morgan with an envelope. The man said, "In my hand I hold a guaranteed formula for success, which I will gladly sell to you for $2,000."

Morgan replied, "I don't know what's in the envelope. However, if you show me and I like it, I give you my word as a gentleman that I will pay you what you ask." The man agreed and handed over the envelope. Morgan opened it, read the contents, and then wrote the man a $2,000 check.

What did the paper say? Two things: One, every morning, write a list of the things that need to be done that day. Two, do them! In that moment, Morgan recognized a plan for a successful day.

Do you have a plan for what you need to accomplish today? If not, that's the first thing you need to commit to.

-58-
Every Moment Matters

Imagine this: It's a championship basketball game. No time left on the clock. Down by just one, the team's superstar steps to the free throw line to take two shots. He gathers himself and shoots. Clank. It bounces off the rim.

No matter. The superstar has one free throw left. Make it and the team can still win in overtime. Again, he gathers himself and shoots. Again, he misses. The game is over. The team loses.

Question: Did the superstar cost his team the championship? Arguably yes. But what about all the other players who missed shots and committed errors throughout the game? Why should the last shot have more intrinsic value to it?

While it might not be fair, that's just the way it is. It's true in business too. Lost deals near a deadline seem to hurt more. The reality is, however, that every moment matters. Take care of the moments in less critical times, and you'll avoid the anxiety of the 11th hour.

-59-
Self-Forgiveness

Gary Wilbers, author of *Cultivate Positive Culture: 10 Actions To Faithful Living*, shared: "True leaders know how to forgive themselves. An important step to being able to do this is to give yourself some time to think and reflect every day."

Wilbers goes on to explain that one of the top habits he instills in the leaders that participate in his executive coaching program is to have a morning routine that involves meditation, prayer, or reflection.

There is certainly merit to this. Life happens fast. Situations require you to quickly think and then act soon thereafter. And that's not a formula for perfect execution. As such, you're going to make mistakes.

However, taking time to reflect allows you to re-assess your decisions and have the grace to understand that you're only human. You did the best you could in the moment, and you're committed to doing better in the future.

-60-
Survivorship Bias

To protect the lives of airmen on bombing raids in World War II, allied forces closely examined planes as they returned to Great Britain from Nazi Germany. As the front and tail wings were heavily riddle with holes, they believed that these were the areas that they needed to reinforce.

The problem is that this sample failed to include the planes that didn't make it back. And those were the ones that provided the most useful information. This is known as the survivorship bias. It's an error of logic, concentrating examination on successes rather than failures, which can lead to false conclusions.

While you aren't flying bombing raids over enemy territory, in life and in business you do experience successes and failures. So, don't just examine the successes, even though it might be euphoric to do so. Chances are your failures hold more insight as to how you can create future wins. So, have the courage to scrutinize them.

-61-
Channel Your Strife

Lee Iacocca, an American automobile executive best known for the development of the Ford Mustang and reviving the Chrysler Corporation as its CEO during the 1980s, once remarked, "In times of great stress or adversity, it's always best to keep busy, to plow your anger and your energy into something positive."

Sure, much of life is rewarding. But life also has its moments where anxiety and hardship rule the day. Or month. Or year. And this is not limited to certain classes of people. No. Difficulties invade the lives of everybody, even heads of state, movie stars and elite professional athletes.

However, not everyone deals with these moments of pain in the same way. Some simply accept it and allow the period of suffering to sour them on others and on life, trapping them in cycles of anger and self-pity.

But as Iacocca shares, the most productive avenue forward is getting busy with professional development, building something lasting or helping others. Channel your strife into constructive ventures.

-62-
Act Into Thinking

Sports psychologist Dr. Rob Bell shared in his book *No One Gets There Alone*:

"If you want to change the way you feel about somebody, change the way you treat them. Changing the way you treat someone takes commitment and action. But it's worth it. The only way to change how we think about others is through action."

As an example, he relates an experience as a graduate student working with the school's collegiate baseball team. The coach simply failed to pay Bell. For years, that made him feel hateful towards the coach. He decided that he did not want to live with that anger.

What did he do? He started sending the coach Christmas cards. Bell shared, "I could not write a Christmas card and hold ill will." This allowed him to let go of his resentment. Bell remarks, "It is easier to act our way into right thinking than it is to think our way into right acting."

-63-
No Charge For Love

One day a farmer posted a sign on his fence advertising puppies for sale. As he did, a cute little boy approached with money in hand saying, "I want to buy one."

Though he did not have enough money the farmer agreed, taken by the young boy's charm. He made a quick whistle. Immediately, a mother dog, with four puppies close behind, raced around the corner. Then a fifth puppy emerged, noticeably lagging behind the rest of the pack. Smaller. Slightly hobbled. It did its best to catch up.

"I want that one," the little boy said, pointing to the runt. The farmer gently chided, "You don't want that one. It'll never be able to play like the others." With that, the boy pulled up his pant legs to reveal steel braces. "Well, I don't run too well myself" he said. "We'll understand each other."

With that, the farmer picked up the tiny pup and handed it to the boy saying, "There's no charge for love."

Take time today to share compassion with another.

-64-
Authentic, Lasting Relationship

At networking events, once you have exchanged names, conversation will likely ensue. Engage in it. This is an important step to building relationships.

However, in so doing, don't start the conversation directly focused on business or professional aspects. That can be off-putting and serve to create an uncomfortable situation. Rather, engage in some small talk.

Inquire as to the origin of their name. Ask them about their impressions on the event itself. Get them talking on anything other than business. This will serve to make the connection comfortable.

After a few (or even) several minutes of small talk, segue over to more professional topics. Ask about their business. How long have they done it? What did they do before? How did they get started?

Once the professional discussion has run its course, segue back to small talk before you go your separate ways. This routine of interacting is an effective means of creating the foundation for an authentic, lasting relationship.

-65-
Needed Versus Valued

Dr. Adam Grant, Wharton School of Business professor and best-selling author, shared on Twitter: "It's nice to be needed, but it's healthier to be valued. Being needed creates dependence: people are helpless without us, so it becomes difficult to say no. Being valued maintains independence: there's no pressure to say yes. Helping becomes a choice, not a chore."

Grant's insight creates an important distinction. Even more important is putting it into action. You create a need for yourself when you get into the habit of just doing for others, swooping in to save the day whenever they require it.

You, however, become valued when you engage in the practice of empowering others, especially with those things they could and should learn to do for themselves.

Think about it. You could continually tie a young child's shoe and be forever needed to do so. Or you could teach them how to do it. This empowers them and frees you up to grow and develop yourself.

-66-
What Do You Want To Know

The key to successful networking is getting lots of great people interested in you. This, however, raises the question, "How do I do that?"

The best way to answer that is to ask yourself this, "What do I want to know about others?" After all, it only makes sense that the reasons why you want to know others would be the same reasons why others would want to know you.

Think about it. What other qualities in people do you admire? Sense of humor? Optimism? Courage? Endeavor to take those on. Become the person you want to network with.

Here's an example. Chances are you cannot help but be impressed by the doers of the world, as those that go the extra mile for company, community or country always seem to have a following. Those are truly the people that everyone – including you – would like to know. So, why not become one?

-67-
Relationship Shifts

It's said, "the only thing that we can count on for sure is change." This is true of almost everything, as change is all around. It even invades your networking initiatives.

Think about it. You create a great relationship with a local business icon. She then decides to take another position across the country. Or you service a client for years. Then, with little warning, they change providers. Or you nurture a relationship with a great center of influence, one who provides you with significant referrals. Then they decide to retire.

Much like everything else in life, relationships are constantly changing or evolving.

What can you do to prevent these relationship shifts? Really nothing. These changes are part of life and are generally beyond your control. And you can't predict where they might happen. So, just accept them.

But at the same time, you can hedge against them. Simply commit to always be forging new relationships. In that sense, make change work for you.

-68-
The Guy Who Knows a Guy

In his book *The Guy Who Knows A Guy*, social architect and professional relationship consultant Michael Whitehouse explains that one of the tactics he used to become uber connected after moving to a small New England town where he knew virtually no one was to encourage people to use him as a resource.

He shares, "Why would I tell people to use me as a resource to get introductions to people they wanted to meet when I barely knew anyone myself?" Whitehouse explains that people like to know people who are a resource. And so, by saying it, that served to expand his network.

He further clarifies that though he knew few people, those few people knew others. And by offering to be a resource to them, he was willing to commit time and energy to find what people were looking for. In short, he became the guy who knew a guy who knew a guy.

-69-
Statements of Character

Thomas Jefferson once said, "You can easily judge the character of a person by how they treat those who can do nothing for them."

As Jefferson was a founding father and third President of the United States, some might argue that the notion of this statement relates to a time long gone by. After all, we now live in a world dominated by business, where transactions are not just common, but almost expected. And how you treat others is somehow related to that.

However, not everything needs to be tied to a *quid pro quo*. You can and should always be willing to lend a hand to others and expect nothing in return. You can and should always be willing to be nice to another human being, no matter who they are.

After all, extending common decency to others is something that should never go out of style. Remember, those actions are statements of character about you.

-70-
Challenges Are Your Opportunities

Thirteenth century Islamic scholar, Jalāl ad-Dīn Muhammad Rūmī – generally referred to simply as Rumi – famously once said, "The wound is the place where the Light enters you."

Everyone suffers from time to time. Some big. Some small. But everyone meets with anguish. This is the wound Rumi refers to. But it is this pain that puts you in a position to reflect. And this reflection then leads to insight. It helps you draw on your reserve of strength. And it leads you to the ways to deal with the pain.

Through these moments you get to test your true capacity. Thus, it's the pain and suffering that help you to grow stronger. This is the light that enters you.

So, it is best to be thankful even in times of adversity. After all, these moments serve to be your greatest teacher. In summary, your challenges are really the gateway to wonderful opportunities.

-71-
Doing Better Than Knowing

Award-winning author and one of "America's Top 100 Thought Leaders", Frank Sonnenberg shared in a December 2020 tweet: "Knowing what's right isn't as important as doing what's right."

This tweet linked to his blog, where he shared an article entitled *Live with Honor and Integrity.* In this short article, he offers insight after insight as to how you can act with virtue. Simple things, like knowing your values, being true to your beliefs, surrounding yourself with noble role models, and the list goes on.

The article and Sonnenberg's tweet imply that it's relatively easy to know what to do. Most everyone knows right from wrong, after all. Where it becomes challenging is standing at the crossroads with two options: One, realizing a personal gain, though compromising your principles in the process. Or, two, doing the right thing even though you must endure a self-sacrifice.

This is the point where doing what's right is better than just knowing what's right.

-72-
Selling With Noble Purpose

In her book *Selling with Noble Purpose: How to Drive Revenue and Do Work That Makes You Proud*, Lisa Earle McLeod revealed that through a six-month long, double-blind study of the sales force at a major biotech firm, the consulting team determined this: The salespeople who cared about something more than just money ended up selling more than the salespeople who were focused only on quota.

In summary, McLeod shares that the mindset that salespeople bring into their customer interactions sets the stage for everything they do. And those with a virtuous purpose (as opposed to mere profit) tend to drive harder for their clients and themselves.

But the notion that a noble mindset drives successful behaviors goes beyond the world of sales. Having a righteous *why* to guide you will serve to make you a better businessperson. A better volunteer. A better community servant. And a better person.

In short, a successful life is so much more than just a *quid pro quo* transaction.

-73-
Have You Given Enough?

In December 2020, author and personal transformation expert Jeff Nischwitz shared on his daily YouTube video insight entitled *BED Talk* about an exchange he had with friends from his corporate career. One person announced he was retiring, to which another person posed two retirement questions. One, do you have enough? And two, have you had enough?

The person responded "Yes," to both questions. Nischwitz, however, posed a third question to ponder: "Have you given enough?"

He went on to share, "I feel this longing inside of me that I have so much more to give, share and impact before I take my last breath. I know this keeps me young in heart, mind, and spirit."

He closes the short video making the point that you end up having enough only when you've done all you can to give enough. In short, what you put into your life somehow comes back to you.

So, have you given enough?

-74-
Selfish Altruism

In his book *Connected: Strategies To Attract the Right Opportunities, Connections and Clients Through Effective Networking*, social architect Terry Bean introduces the term "selfish altruism." In so doing, he shares:

"I love seeing these two words - 'selfish' and 'altruism'- butted up against one another. They seem so contrary, don't they? And yet when you practice networking, you really are practicing the ideology embraced when these two words collide. Networking allows you to get what you want (selfish) by helping others get what they want (altruism)."

Bean's term mimics an academic definition of networking which characterizes the practice as "short-term generosity with long-term self-interest." In short, it's the habit of adding value to those around you, while at the same time trusting that benefits will accrue to you eventually.

Bean's selfish altruism is also in line with the well-known Hindu term, *karma*. Whatever term you prefer, do something for another today.

-75-
Thoughtful Awareness

A consistent mantra of networking is that if you want to get things from those in your network, we need to give first. But to totally surrender to the notion that "givers get," you need to focus and act upon ways in which you can be considerate of the feelings of others.

It's the little things. For example, allowing someone to go ahead of you in line, even though it might delay you a tad.

Or things that might go unnoticed, like gravitating towards the person in the room that looks as if they feel out of place.

By looking for little things, you've primed your mind to be ready to spot the bigger ones too. So, in time, you're able to act upon larger deeds – like spotting a great referral for someone or making an introduction.

Whatever the case, this thoughtful awareness will come back to you. In big ways and small ways. In ways you cannot even imagine.

-76-
Verbal Essays

An important part of building relationships is the seemingly mundane small talk conversation that serves to kick off human interaction. It's also something that trips many up because they are never sure what to say.

Know this: It's not about what you have to say. It's about what you get the other person to say. Seriously! If you are interested in effectively carrying on a conversation, it is vital to keep the other person talking.

The trick to doing this is arming yourself with open-ended questions rather than questions requiring only a one- or two-word answer. That is, be prepared to give your small talk partner an opening to share a verbal essay.

For example, a question like "What did you do this week?" has more staying power than "How was your weekend?", which is usually followed by "Fine", "OK" or "Pretty good." The first question, in contrast, allows them to really share and also leads to other questions, allowing you to show a genuine interest.

-77-
Mental Re-Wiring

In his book *The Power of Optimism: Attitude Training for Those Who Want More from Life*, leadership psychologist Tim Shurr makes the point that the things you think about most, your subconscious mind works to create. "What you think about comes about." Based on this insight, he offers a four-step strategy for re-wiring your mind:

Step One: Become more aware of what you're saying to yourself, as what you say to yourself will determine how you feel. This in turn, drives your responses to other people, situations, and events.

Step Two: When you catch yourself talking to yourself in a negative fashion – for example, "I'm not good at small talk" – stop yourself. Challenge the thought – for example, "That's simply not true."

Step Three: Building on the challenge in Step Two, quickly replace the negative thought with a positive thought. For example, a replacement thought might be, "I'm getting better and better at making small talk."

And finally, Step Four: Practice and repeat the first three steps.

-78-
Everybody Is Human

In his book Bo: Life, Laughs, and Lessons of a College Football Legend, iconic University of Michigan football coach Bo Schembechler shared a valuable lesson that he learned through his son, Chip. Though not spectacular, his son played high school football. Before one game, his son's coach told Chip to give up his equipment so that the star player could be better outfitted.

This really struck Schembechler. So much so, that the Hall of Fame coach vowed to always supply every player – whether walk-on or destined for NFL greatness – with their own full uniform including their name sewn on the back of the jersey.

That might seem like a small gesture. But it sent a message to the player – and likely to their parents in the stands – that you are important and are part of this team.

With your team, even if it's just a small business or department, remember that everyone is human. Treat them as such.

-79-
Support Their Dreams

Networking is about helping others and then trusting that in time they will help you in return. By that definition, it starts with you. You need to take the initiative to do something for someone else.

Certainly, there are lots of things that you can do for others. Make introductions. Give referrals for business. Share opportunities and information that can benefit them. And even support them on social media with likes and comments.

In helping others, however, remember that not all assistance is created equal. And that the most impactful support you can provide are the things that serve to advance their dreams and aspirations.

Sure, this takes a little extra effort. You need to really learn about what they want to accomplish. And moreover, you need to understand what they want to be known for. But it's this little extra effort that positions you to provide them lasting value. And it's this effort that makes an indelible memory in their mind about you.

-80-
Boost Knowledge

In his book *MORE: Word of Mouth Referrals, Lifelong Customers and Raving Fans*, word-of-mouth referral consultant Matt Ward shares,

"Although your contacts know that learning about their industries will enhance their knowledge and ultimately make them better businesspeople, they rarely take time to do this. Why? Because they're too busy delivering their products and services to their customers. What's the solution? Do the research for them."

Ward goes on to advocate that you devote 10 minutes each week researching an industry-related article or information for just one contact. Then share it with them. This doesn't take much effort, but it will help the people you know in a small but meaningful way.

As Ward wraps up this segment of his book he shares, "I have done this consistently over the years and I always get great feedback from my contacts. They clearly appreciate that I went above and beyond for them."

-81-
Set the World Ablaze

Catherine of Siena was a 14th century author and lay member of the Dominican Order who had a great influence on Italian literature. She once remarked "If you are what you should be, you will set the world ablaze."

So, what's stopping you from becoming what you should be? The Internet gives you access to the collective knowledge of mankind since the beginning of recorded time. You have the ability to move about, reaching any corner of the world - physically in mere days and virtually in just seconds. The advent of electricity enables you to work at any hour of the day or night. And medical breakthroughs allow you to live a long, healthy, productive life.

So, what limitation do you really have? If there are any, they're likely between your ears, as you can conquer literally anything you can envision and are willing to diligently pursue.

Therefore, heed the words of Catherine of Siena: Become all you should become. And light the world with your presence.

-82-
The FORD System

In one of his weekly newsletters, Mark Given, author, speaker, and innovator of the trust-based philosophy, wrote about Socrates.

Given shared that Socrates would pose a simple question to lead his students into deep vibrant discussions. Known as the Socratic Method, it encourages engagement and learning and is especially effective when people can talk about something they love.

Given then suggested that you use these same principles to build relationships in the 21st century. To do this, ask questions using the FORD system. F. O. R. D.

F is for Family: Ask a question or simply direct the conversation to the other person's family.

O is for Occupation: Find out where they work and what they do.

R is Recreation: Hit on topics that let them talk about what they do for fun.

And D is for Dreams: What do they aspire to?

According to Given, the FORD system can serve to build trust and bolster your relationships.

-83-
Focus On What You Can Do

In his book *Small Ball Big Results*, Joel Goldberg, veteran broadcaster for the Kansas City Royals, shared a heartwarming story of Jeff Hanson — a young man born with a genetic condition that ultimately led to his vision being somewhat impaired. While Hanson could not see, he had a creative gift. He could paint.

And paint he did. Over the years, he created masterpieces that were commissioned by and proudly hang on the walls of people like Bill Gates, Billie Jean King, and George Lucas. But beyond a mere business, Hanson used his talents to raises millions for medical research charities.

As part of the story, Goldberg shared an insightful quote from Hanson's father which, in part, reads: "Focus on what you can do, not what you can't do."

Think on that one today. What are your strengths? What do you do really well? Those are the things you need to double down on. Those are the things the world needs most from you.

-84-
Do You Know What Tomorrow Is?

No one has ever had such a wonderful life that they have not endured a setback or experienced a bad day. After all, bad luck happens. It rains on everyone's world at some point. For everyone, missteps occur. And at times metaphorical self-inflicted wounds mark people's not-so-great moments. But no matter the situation, do you know what tomorrow is? It's another day.

It's true. No matter what became of today, tomorrow is another one. Darkness will descend. The stars will shine. The night will pass. Then the sun will rise, and you will have another chance to start over.

No, you can't undo the past. But whatever happened, whether happenstance or intentional, merely marks your starting point for this new day. And while you cannot simply erase yesterday from your history, you can always start forward from it.

You can set forth with a steely resolve that says, "I'm still here. I'm undeterred. And I'm unstoppable. This is a new day!"

-85-
Altruistic Income

If you're looking for more opportunities and advantages in your professional life, consider volunteering. Now, you might be thinking: "Volunteer? I am not looking for another distraction or drain on my already limited time."

Listen, volunteering is neither a disruption nor an idle consumption of your time. Think about it. Groups and organizations need the foundational skills and capabilities you have. Through volunteer opportunities, those skills will be utilized in ways that serve to expand your experiences beyond what you'd see in a typical workday. And this adds to the value you bring to your clients or employer.

Plus, when you volunteer, you aren't doing so all alone. Volunteering pulls you out of your world and thrusts you shoulder-to-shoulder with others who are doing the same good work. And these new contacts fortify and diversify your network, further enhancing your value to those who rely on you.

So, volunteering – at any level, for any organization – is one activity where you can both give and get at the same time.

-86-
Clock Or Compass?

In his book *Cultivate Positive Culture: 10 Actions to Faithful Living*, Gary Wilbers, professional speaker and host of the Charge podcast, asks whether you live by the clock or by the compass? He shares:

"Too many people live their life by the clock and not by a compass. The correlation is simple: The clock is about time; the compass is about direction. Do you live by time or direction? Are you so busy completing tasks that each day is a race? If you live by direction, what guides you?

Wilber's question is largely rhetorical. You are not on this earth to idly pass the time while waiting to die. Rather, you're here to add value to others. And to do that you need a purposeful plan, which implies living by direction.

To make this a reality, Wilbers goes on to encourage you to view your life as offering a message to others. That message should be largely timeless, but it will guide your direction.

-87-
You Get to Give

A consistent message in the world of building relationships is that you need to add value to others in the manner they need. And then trust that the goodness you've put into the world will come back to you in a manner that somehow serves you. In short, if you want to get things from those in your network, you need to resolve to give first.

So, if you are already focused on giving in order to get from our network, great. But the fact of the matter is that if this is the only reason you are giving, you are only halfway home. You see, the "give to get" mindset implies a calculated *quid pro quo* notion.

To totally surrender to the true spirit of networking, you must elevate your mindset to another level. You need to give and add value simply because it's the right thing to do. In short, you no longer give to get, but rather you get to give.

-88-
Can You Introduce Me To...?

Think of all the people you know. People from high school. People from college. People from a litany of career steps. People from your volunteer efforts. And this list could go on. It's impressive to think about all the people you know.

Now ponder this: What about all the people your network is connected to that you've not yet met? That number is staggering. But also exciting at the same time. After all, many of those potential new contacts could benefit you in lots of ways. Referrals. Information. Opportunities. And still more contacts.

The point is that the people you know are gateways to a treasure trove of others. How do you meet them? Simple: Ask.

Most people are more than happy to introduce you to others. Remember, they want others to perceive them as a connector. Moreover, at some point they might need the same favor. So, simply turn to someone you know and ask, "Can you introduce me to...?"

-89-
Right Mindset; Right Moment

Pam Christian, host of *The Juice* podcast has a mantra, "The right mindset at the right moment changes everything."

The motivational speaker and mindset coach goes on to share that you have the ability to change your reality by changing your thought patterns relative to the status quo. Whether you're dealing with tragedy, ongoing challenges in your world, or your life just not all you want it to be, you're empowered to alter things.

But it starts with you. It starts with how you view the situation. And how you think about yourself relative to it and others.

So, what do you want in life? Do you want to lift yourself up from a traumatic experience? Do you want to feel like you belong in a community or group? Do you want to feel as if you're enjoying more business success? You can answer yes to all of those and more. The right moment is now, and the right mindset starts with believing in yourself.

-90-
You Just Never Know

Human connections are full of surprises. You just never know when that someone in your network will do something that will have a positive impact on your business, career, or personal life.

You just never know. Someone might bestow upon you an opportunity – seemingly simple and small – that serves to make your day more productive, profitable, or enjoyable.

You just never know. A casual conversation with someone whom you've never met before can yield information or insight that converts what was shaping up to be a complex problem into a simple solution.

You just never know. Perhaps someone you've known for years pops back into your life to refer you a client or a key employee that vaults you to a record month, quarter or year.

You just never know. And for that reason alone, you need to make building relationships with those around you a consistent practice. Why? Because you just never know.

-91-
An Inspiring Life Story

Great stories move people. They stir emotions. They solidify opinions. They serve to inspire conviction and motivate action.

Given that, what story are you writing with your life? If your story isn't inspiring to you, then it probably isn't going to move anyone else either. If your story doesn't jolt you out of bed to take on the day, who do you expect that it will jolt out of bed? No one, that's who.

So, if you're not happy with your story, perhaps it's time to pay attention to it. You can start today by metaphorically writing a sentence through your intentions and actions. That then continues tomorrow with another metaphorical sentence. In time, you will have created a paragraph. Then after several months, you will have crafted a chapter that serves to inspire others. From there, you're on your way.

Life is best when you live it in a fashion that creates an inspiring story, one that intrigues others and challenges them to rethink their own lives.

-92-
Do Good Everywhere

Brian Reinbold, host of the *Braveheart Radio Show* has a mantra: "Doing good anywhere is doing good everywhere."

Reinbold, as the Mission Specialist for Braveheart For Kids which provides life-saving hope and inspiration to families facing a pediatric cancer ordeal, explains the mantra like this: "If you'd prefer to support another cause – homelessness, hunger, literacy, whatever – that's fine by me. I cannot help but believe that somehow that goodness will serve to benefit our mission in time."

No one … and nothing … exists in isolation. The whole world is connected. When someone is suffering, we all suffer. When someone is doing well, it spills over into everyone's life – directly or indirectly.

With that understanding, however you doing good in the world serves to impact everyone somehow. So, don't get caught up trying to determine the highest and best use of your efforts. Rather just devote that energy to doing good. Anywhere. As that serves to do good everywhere.

-93-
Meeting of the Minds

George Bernard Shaw, a 20th century playwriter and political activist, once remarked that, "The single biggest problem in communication is the illusion that it has taken place."

Shaw's quote should cause you to reflect. Sure, you share thoughts and commentary, both written and verbal. And sure, the intent of your message is abundantly clear to you. The question is how can you be sure that your message resonated with the person you're conversing with?

And likewise, people share with you their thoughts and commentary. Again, both written and verbal. Sure, you can read or hear the words. And while people intend a message that is clear to them, is it clear to you?

Both these situations underscore the ultimate test of communication. With whomever you converse, and however you converse, you need ensure that not only do the words of the message come through, but also the intent behind them. It's when you have this meeting of the minds that communication really happens.

-94-
Small Talk Science

Let's face it ... small talk has a bad reputation. Far too often people see it as idle chitchat that has no productive value in the professional world. This, however, could not be more wrong. Both social science studies and neuroscience experimentation have shown that this seemingly nonsensical banter has incredible value in building relationships with others.

You see, the biology of the human brain is such that the mind is constantly seeking out shortcuts to complex problems. One such problem is the immense complexity regarding whether or not to trust someone.

It seems, however, that friendly small talk – yes, that meaningless, idle chitchat – creates a signal in the human brain that gives others the green light to trust you.

No, this doesn't guarantee that you will completely win them over with the utterance of "How about that game last night?" But something like that gives you a foothold in creating a wonderful relationship. And from there, there is a world of possibilities.

-95-
Two Important Roles

In his book *Connected: Strategies To Attract the Right Opportunities, Connections and Clients Through Effective Networking*, social architect Terry Bean shares:

"As an individual inside of a network we have two important jobs. We need to know who we look to meet and communicate our needs. And we have to know what value we have to offer to the network. Neither is more important than the other. They are in fact driven by the needs of the individual and the network at any given moment."

In short, Bean's words encourage you to be ever ready to help those in your network. Certainly, friends and family. But also, co-workers, colleagues, vendors, and even competitors. Anyone with whom you want to have a positive and productive relationship.

But at the same time Bean reminds that you have needs too. And thus, you also need to be willing to ask of your network. You need to fulfill both these important roles for the networking process to work effectively.

-96-
Electrify Others

Whether you know it or not, you've got influence. The people around you are subconsciously observant of your every move. When you smile, others smile. When you cross your arms, others are likely to, as well. You let out a yawn, the people around you will too. You've got influence.

While it's nice to know that you can get others to smile, cross their arms, or yawn, that's not the highest and best use of the impact you have on others. You can use this invisible power to light up your network.

Think about it. When you're enthusiastic, you tend to bring out enthusiasm in others. It's true. When you are full of energy, you inspire the energy in others. Again, you have influence. It's like your enthusiasm and energy are contagious.

This does not mean you have to be loud, excited, or gregarious. However, when you're confident, passionate, and optimistic, this serves to electrify others.

-97-
Initiating Relationships

No matter how great a network you might have, you need to always devote a degree of time adding people to it. It's a fact of life, as relationships tend to ebb and flow for everyone.

As everything has a beginning, so do relationships. And 99 times out of 100 they start with a mundane conversation about ... well ... everyday things. News. Sports. Weather. The state of the coffee in your hand.

There is no special skill required to kicking off this small talk banter. It can be initiated as simply as saying hello to anyone who makes eye contact and seeing what comes from that. Or at an event, introducing yourself to anyone not actively engaged in conversation.

Here's the thing. If you want new relationships in your world, then initiating conversation is 100 percent your obligation. You can't expect anyone else to do it. It's totally on you.

You need these relationships to become successful. So, what are you waiting for?

-98-
Wildest Dreams

In the March-April 2020 issue of *Success Magazine*, Lewis Howes, author, speaker, and host of *The School of Greatness* podcast, offers three tips for achieving your wildest dreams.

One, you have to put aside a play-it-safe mentality. Howes shares "What feels like a negative turning point can become your greatest success. If you play it safe, you'll never know."

Two, believe in greatness. Think bigger than you've ever thought before. Sure, this is no doubt much easier said than done. Even Howes acknowledges that. But he encourages you to ponder this: What does believing in yourself look like?"

Finally, lead with authenticity. That is, be you. Howes, a renowned lifestyle entrepreneur shares, "When it comes to promoting yourself or your business, if it feels icky, it probably is. If it doesn't feel like you, it probably isn't."

If you're going to dream about a better life, why shoot for just a little bit better. Why not a lot better? What would be your wildest dream? Now, go for it.

-99-
Fix Flaws

People are flawed. You're flawed. We're all flawed. Sure, some flaws are more glaring than others, but flaws are just part of the human experience. However, everyone contends with other people's flaws differently.

Some people see the flaws in others and accept them. For this, they are no better or no worse. And neither is the flawed person.

Other people see someone's flaw and become judgmental. Inwardly and, at times, outwardly they're critical of this person's intentions and abilities. In so doing, these people serve to temporarily improve their relative value, taking solace in the notion that they're not flawed in that way.

But then there are those who see a flaw in another, and then work to help that person overcome it somehow. That person not only improves the life of another, but they also serve to permanently raise their absolute value.

When you see a flaw in another, work to help them. We're all flawed, but we all want to be better too.

-100-
Look In the Mirror

In his book *The Power of Positivity: Controlling Where the Ball Bounces*, international professional speaker Cornell Thomas remarks, "Believing in yourself isn't arrogance; it's common sense."

He goes on to share about his brother, Rob, who is a successful life coach and can motivate anyone in a matter of minutes. Thomas writes, "I've always said if everyone had someone like Rob walking around with them every day imagine all the great things that could be accomplished on this earth. The funny thing is we all do walk around with that person; it's who we see in the mirror."

Consider Thomas' thought. Chances are you glance at yourself in the mirror a few times every day – even just to check your looks. Try this. Instead of a quick glance, take a good look in the mirror, staring directly into your own eyes and tell yourself this.

"I believe in you. You've got this. Today, you're going to do great things."

Form this habit, and positive change will follow.

-101-
Four Times Four Equals

Four times four equals 16. Two times eight equals 16. And the square root of 256 is 16. There are lots of paths to the number 16. And none of them is better than the other. Sure, arguably one might seem easier than the next, but they each get you to the same place.

The same is true of success. There is not just one way. So, don't let that unsolicited someone emphatically tell you that you should or should not be doing this or that to accomplish your dreams.

Sure, take note of what others are doing and saying. Seek input and advice. And politely listen. But in the end, whatever you aim to do is in your hands. And you know your unique situation best.

So, metaphorically speaking, you need to decide whether the path to achievement for you is going to be via two times eight or four times four.

There you have it—101 essays. But we wanted to offer a bonus essay. Before we do, if you're interested in exploring other books, content, and programs by Frank Agin, visit frankagin.com or simply search "Frank Agin" on whatever platform you use to get great content.

-102-
Me Mad ... Me Reframe

Marvel Comics' character the Hulk often remarked in a very primitive voice: "Hulk mad; Hulk smash." And then he carries about in a fit of rage destroying things ... lots of things. But that's just a caricature of the human condition, right? You get mad. You want to lash out. And you're not alone.

But in his *Think Again* series Dr. Adam Grant offers insight into human anger and how to better control it. He shares:

"Getting mad is a signal that something important to you is at risk. Understanding what makes you angry is a prism for understanding what you value."

Grant goes on to explain that if you stop in a moment of anger to rationalize why you feel threatened, you'll quell the wrath building within. This is known as 'reframing.' And it allows you to turn off the Hulk rage portion of your brain. In so doing, you can turn yourself back into mild mannered Dr. Bruce Banner.

About The Author

Frank Agin is president of AmSpirit Business Connections, which empowers entrepreneurs, sales representatives, and professionals to become successful and gain more referrals through networking.

He also shares information and insights on professional relationships, business networking and best practices for generating referrals on his Networking Rx podcast and through various professional programs.

Finally, Frank is the author of several books, including *Foundational Networking: Building Know, Like & Trust to Create a Life of Extraordinary Success*. See all his books and programs at frankagin.com. You can reach him at frankagin@amspirit.com.

www.ingramcontent.com/pod-product-compliance
Lightning Source LLC
Chambersburg PA
CBHW040757220326
41597CB00029BB/4968